HARD DRIVE BOY

by Jonny Zucker
illustrated by Paul Savage

Titles in Full Flight 6

Hard Drive Boy	Jonny Zucker
Robot Safe Crackers	Jonny Zucker
Blood Wheels	Stan Cullimore
Surf Attack	Alison Hawes
The Dream Catcher	Jane A.C. West
Framed!	Jillian Powell
House of Fear	Tony Norman
Go-Kart Crazy	Roger Hurn
Spirit Tribe	Melanie Joyce
Lunar Rover	David Orme

Badger Publishing Limited
15 Wedgwood Gate, Pin Green Industrial Estate,
Stevenage, Hertfordshire SG1 4SU
Telephone: 01438 356907. Fax: 01438 747015.
www.badger-publishing.co.uk
enquiries@badger-publishing.co.uk

Hard Drive Boy ISBN 978-1-84691-661-8

Text © Jonny Zucker 2009
Complete work © Badger Publishing Limited 2009

All rights reserved. No part of this publication may be reproduced, stored in any form or by any means mechanical, electronic, recording or otherwise without the prior permission of the publisher.

The right of Jonny Zucker to be identified as author of this Work has been asserted by him in accordance with the Copyright, Designs and Patents Act 1988.

Series Editor: Jonny Zucker
Publisher: David Jamieson.
Editor: Danny Pearson
Design: Fi Grant
Cover illustration: Paul Savage

Contents

Chapter 1 **Dan Lash** page 4
Chapter 2 **Ball Boy** page 9
Chapter 3 **Freaky Friend** page 14
Chapter 4 **Water Dive** page 20
Chapter 5 **Be There!** page 24
Chapter 6 **The Face Off** page 27

Badger Publishing

Chapter 1
Dan Lash

The piece of paper hit Nick Hall on the back of the head. He turned round and saw the grinning faces of school "hard-man" Jed Frame and his best mate Tom Bolt.

It was last lesson of the day; maths.

"Loser," mouthed Jed.

Tom laughed.

Nick groaned and shook his head. Jed was a total pain. He was always on Nick's case.

When Nick got home he went to his bedroom. He slumped into his chair and flicked on his computer.

The graphics for his favourite game - Jungle Killers 3 - flashed across the screen.
Nick could forget about Jed Frame when he was playing Jungle Killers 3.

The hero of the game, a jungle warrior called Dan Lash, appeared on the screen.

"What's up?" asked Dan, staring straight into Nick's eyes.

Nick sat up in shock.

"I said, what's up?" asked Dan.

Nick rubbed his eyes. "You...you just spoke," he whispered to the face on the screen.

But before Nick could say anything else, there was a flash of white light from the screen. One second later, Dan Lash was standing in Nick's room.

"You have come out of the computer!" said Nick.

"Yeah," nodded Dan. "You looked unhappy, so I came to see what is wrong."

"It's this kid called Jed Frame," said Nick. "He is always on at me."

"Where can we find him?" asked Dan. Nick checked his watch. "He will be at the park now."

Dan walked to the door. "So what are we waiting for?" he asked.

Chapter 2
Ball Boy

Nick took a football to the park. When he and Dan got there Jed Frame was not around. So they had an ice cream from a van.

"This is way better than any of the food in Jungle Killers 3!" said Dan.

Next, Nick and Dan started playing football.

Nick was good but Dan was great. He knew all sorts of tricks and flicks.

"I picked these skills up from the lads in the game Football 360," said Dan.

Ten minutes later, Jed Frame and Tom Bolt showed up.

"Who is your freaky friend?" shouted Jed.

"My name is Dan," shouted Dan. "How about us two versus you two in football?"

"OK," nodded Jed. He walked over and grabbed the ball.

But instead of playing a match he booted it high in the air. It landed on top of some flats.

"Losers!" shouted Jed. Tom laughed.

But Dan was already running incredibly fast towards the flats.

He went round the back and a minute later came out with the ball.

Jed, Tom and Nick were amazed.

"How did you do that?" asked Tom.

"He must have had another ball round there," sneered Jed. "How pathetic!"

"How about that football match?" asked Dan.

"No way!" said Jed. "I am not playing with you and your freaky fricnd."

And with that Jed and Tom headed off.

"That was brilliant!" grinned Nick.

Dan looked back at him.
"That was nothing," he said.

Chapter 3
Freaky Friend

In school the next day, Jed threw another piece of paper at Nick's head. Nick turned round.

"You and your freaky friend better watch it," said Jed with an evil stare.

"Or what?" asked Nick.

"Or you will be facing this!"

Jed clenched his fist.

At that second a piece of paper flew in the window and smacked Jed on the side of his head.

Nick looked round, saw a hand disappearing from the window ledge and heard Dan Lash's laugh.

"Who did that?" demanded Jed.

But no one said anything.

Nick grinned. Having Dan Lash around was starting to be a lot of fun.

After school, Nick and Dan cycled over to the river.

Nick had borrowed his older brother's bike for Dan.

"It was great when you threw that piece of paper through the window at Jed's head," laughed Nick.

"I knew you'd like it," said Dan.

When they got to the river, they sat eating chocolate and skimming stones into the water.

Dan told Nick loads of tricks for Jungle Killers 3.

"Soon you'll be the best player on earth!" laughed Dan.

"Look who it is!" said a voice suddenly.

Nick and Dan looked round. It was Jed and Tom.

Nick groaned. "Not them again!" he hissed.

Jed and Tom walked over.

"What are you and your freaky friend doing?" snapped Jed.

"Leave us alone!" shouted Nick.

"Oh, I am scared!" mocked Jed.

The next second Jed grabbed Nick's bag off the ground.

"Say goodbye to it!" Jed laughed.

Jed threw the bag far into the water.

It floated off to a place where the water suddenly became very fast.

In a few seconds his bag would be smashed to pieces.

Chapter 4
Water Dive

"See you around losers!" grinned Jed as he and Tom cycled off laughing.

"Nightmare!" said Nick. "That has got all of my school stuff and my phone and my MP3 player in!"

"Don't worry," said Dan.

Dan looked around to make sure no one was looking. He dived into the river.

Nick watched in amazement as Dan swum at incredible speed towards the bag and the gushing water.

For a moment, Dan disappeared from sight and Nick thought he had drowned.

But two seconds later, Dan's head popped up. He held Nick's bag in the air.

Dan then swam back to the edge of the water at top speed.

Nick saw that Dan was not wet at all. But Nick's bag was soaking.

He opened it. His books were very wet but he could see that they would dry ok and luckily, his phone and MP3 player worked ok.

Then Nick had an idea. "Come on!" he shouted at Dan. "Let's go!"

Dan ran after him and they both got on their bikes.

They pedalled very fast and five minutes later saw Jed Frame and Tom up ahead.

"Let's go for it!" shouted Nick.

Nick and Dan sped up and whooshed past Jed and Tom. Nick's bag was firmly on his back.

Jed and Tom were astonished to see the bag.

Their mouths fell open but they said nothing.

Chapter 5
Be There!

At lunchtime the next day, Jed came up to Nick in the playground.

"I'm sick of you and your freaky friend!" snapped Jed. "So I have a plan. You two will fight me and Tom behind the supermarket after school."

"If you win we will leave you alone; if we win you will have to bring money to school every Monday and give it to me."

"But I..."

"There are no buts!" hissed Jed.

"Just be there!"

When Nick got home he told Dan everything.

"We have to be there at six o'clock."

Nick was not worried about the fight. Dan Lash was a great fighter so Jed and Tom would get a shock.

But Nick was in for a shock himself.

"I'm really sorry," said Dan, "but I have to go back into the computer. I will get ill if I stay out here for any longer."

Nick felt his heart sink. Now he would have to face Jed and Tom alone. He did not stand a chance.

Chapter 6
The Face Off

At six o'clock Nick showed up behind the supermarket.

Jed and Tom were there.

"Where is your freaky friend?" shouted Jed.

"He is not coming," replied Nick. "It is me against you two."

Jed and Tom burst out laughing. "OK," grinned Jed, "you will not last a second."

But as they ran towards Nick and lashed out with their fists, he blocked their punches and threw them onto the ground.

They got up and kicked out at him.

He blocked their feet and high-kicked them both to the ground.

They cried out in pain and looked very scared.

"That was from me and my freaky friend!" Nick shouted.

Jed's bottom lip trembled.

"We will leave you alone from now on!" he said, "please don't hurt us!"

Nick snarled at them.

Jed and Tom scrambled to their feet and ran away.

Back home, Nick flicked on Jungle Killers 3.

Dan Lash's face appeared.

"How did it go?" asked Dan.

"Because you taught me those fight moves before you went back into the computer, it was easy!" grinned Nick.

"Will you be coming out again some time?"

"Definitely," replied Dan, "but there is one thing you could do for me."

"What is it?"

"Can you make sure you have lots of that ice-cream in your freezer?

The food in here is still terrible!"